This igloo book belongs to:

....

igloobooks

Illustrated by Daniel Howarth
Written by Alex Michaels

Cover designed by Lee Italiano
Interiors designed by Jason Shortland
Edited by Natalia Boileau

Copyright © 2017 Igloo Books Ltd

An imprint of Igloo Books Group,
a Bonnier Publishing company
www.bonnierpublishing.com

Published in 2018
by Igloo Books Ltd, Cottage Farm
Sywell, NN6 0BJ
All rights reserved, including the right of reproduction
in whole or in part in any form.

Manufactured in China. STA002 0618
10 9 8 7 6 5 4 3 2

Library of Congress Cataloging-in-Publication
Data is available upon request.

ISBN 978-1-78810-068-7
IglooBooks.com
www.bonnierpublishing.com

Just the Way You Are

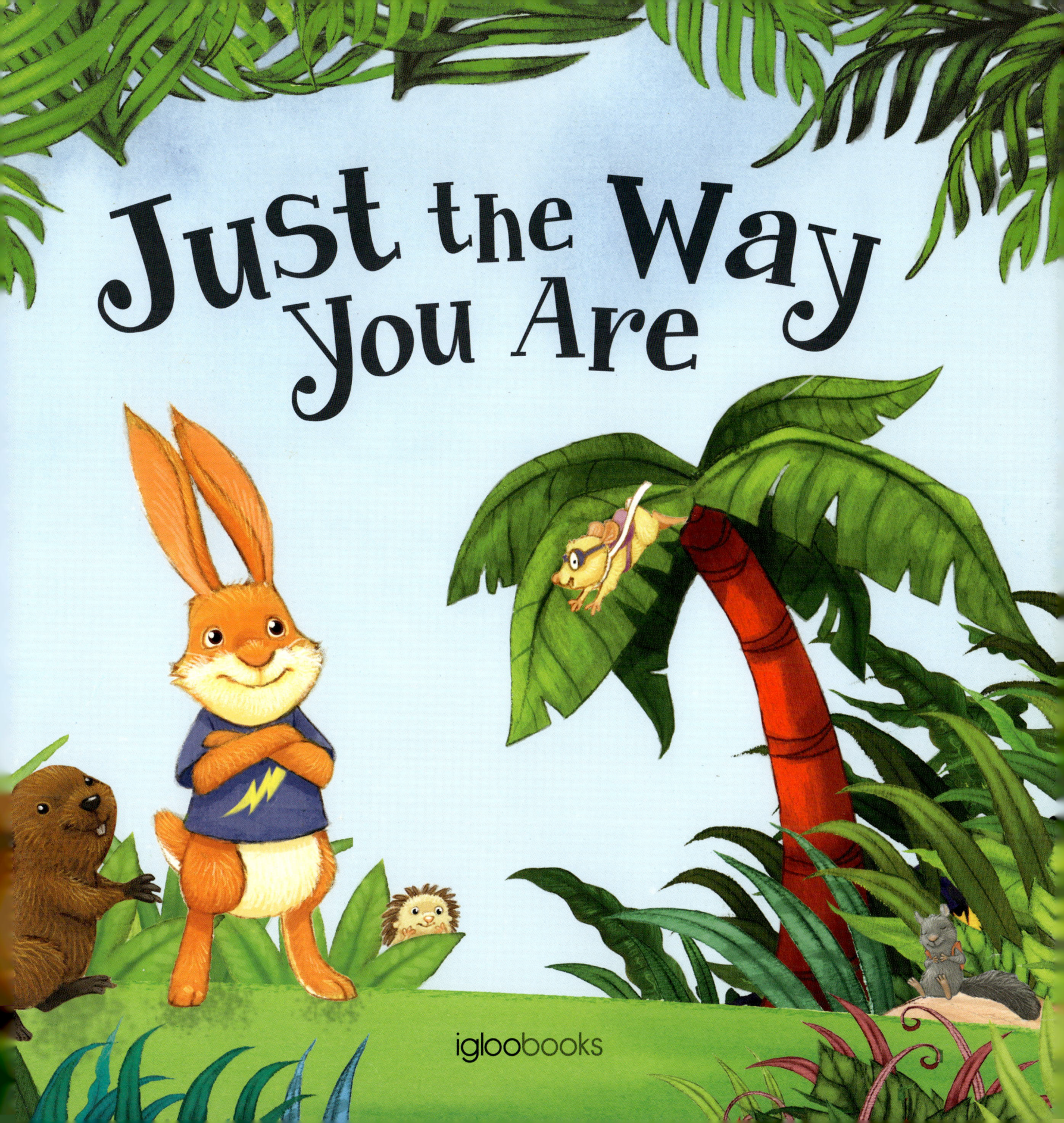

igloobooks

To Mouse

Even though we're different, I think that you're a star.
In fact, you're simply **perfect**, just the way you are.

I am fast and you are slow, but we have *fun* together.

We **always** go outside and play,
no matter what the weather.

I know that friends like us make a very unlikely pair.

I just **want** you to know
that I really, truly care.

I was wondering why I **like** you and now I can see why. It's because you make me so happy, I feel like I can **fly**.

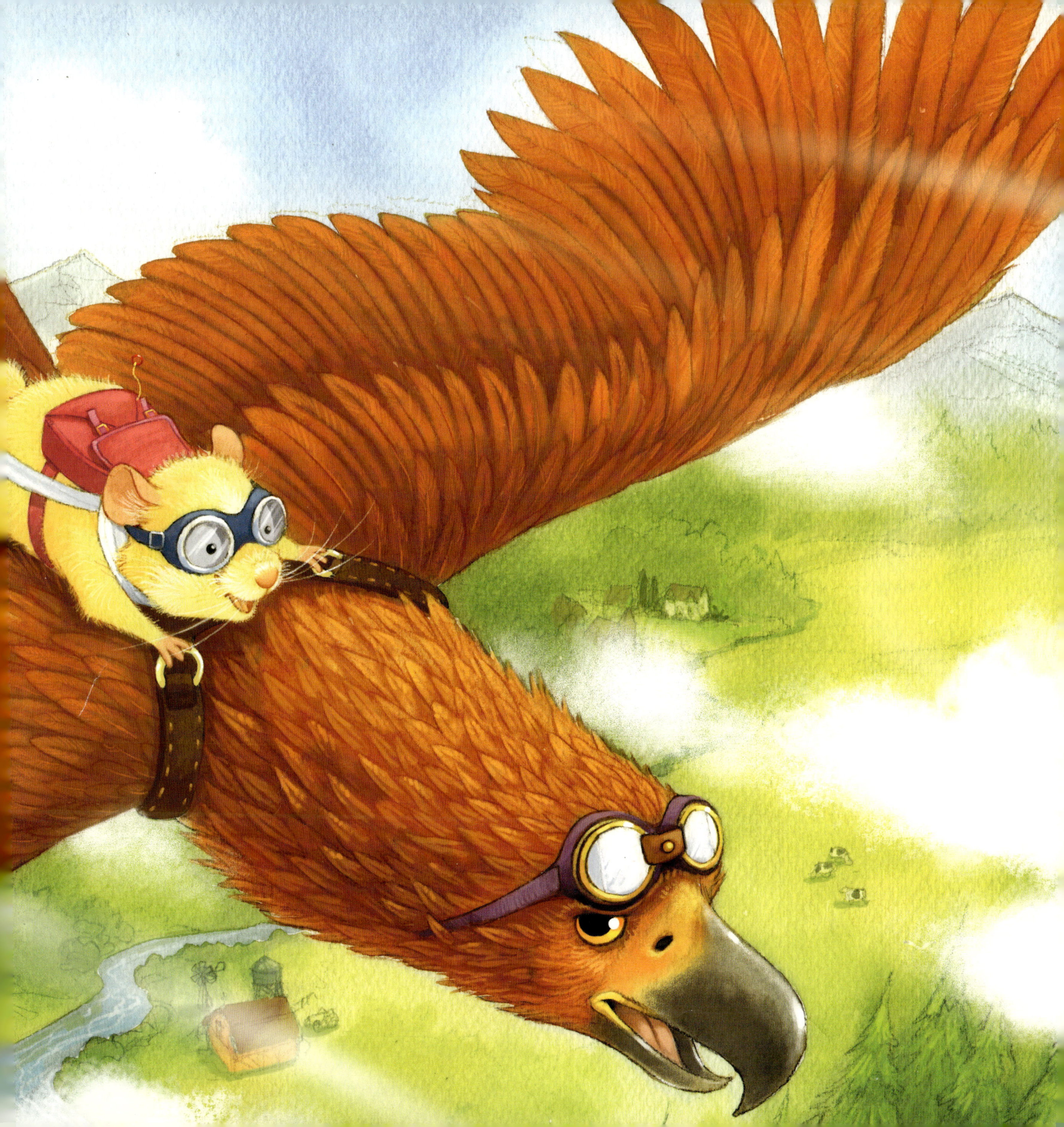

Even though you're **spiky**, you've got a **heart** of gold.

I **hope** that we'll be friends until we're **really** old.

Sometimes you're very **silly**, but I **love** you all the same.

The **best** time of the day is when we play our *special* game.

I'm not sure **why** I like you.
It must be all your **charm**.

Sometimes you can be **scary**, but I know I'm **safe** from harm.

Even though we like different things, I **love** you anyway.

You're the **only** one I want to play with every day.

I just want to say to you that I'm **proud** you are my friend.

We may not be the **same,** but we'll make it in the end.

Others might think it's *funny* when they see us together.
We just **smile** because we know we'll be friends forever.

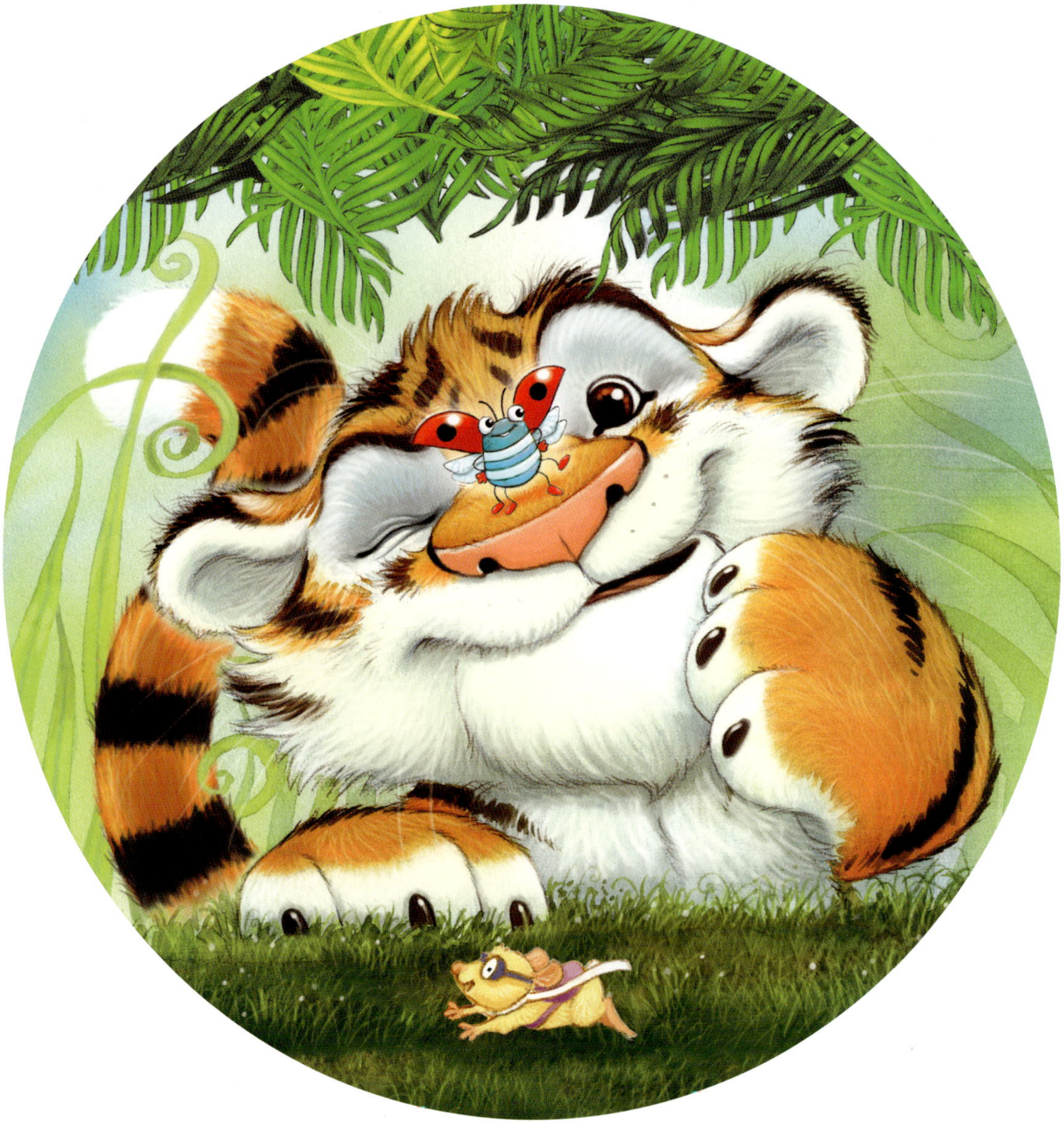